WEST WALES RAILWAYS

WHITLAND TO PEMBROKE DOCK

WEST WALES RAILWAYS

WHITLAND TO PEMBROKE DOCK

JOHN HODGE

PEN & SWORD
TRANSPORT

AN IMPRINT OF PEN & SWORD BOOKS LTD.
YORKSHIRE – PHILADELPHIA

Front cover: The Pembroke Coast Express was the prime service on the branch and here Carmarthen's 7825 Lechlade Manor is seen with the five coach train at Whitland on 8th May 1963. At Swansea a Dining Portion of three vehicles will be added to make the train up to eight coaches for the journey on to Paddington. (Colour Rail)

Back cover top: Whitland had several examples of 2-6-2 tanks of the 45XX, 41XX and 61XX series, often with an 81XX, allocated. Here their 6114 departs Whitland for Pembroke Dock with the remaining three coach portion of the 8.55am ex-Paddington, now running under B headcode lamps on 31st August 1962. (W.G. Sumner)

Back cover bottom: The ultimate in modernity on the branch is shown in this shot of one of the new Class 800 IETs now cleared to work on the branch and seen here near Narberth on the Summer Saturdays 8.45am from Paddington on 8th June 2019. (Stephen Miles)

Title page: Manor No. 7814 *Fringford Manor* between Templeton and Kilgetty with a four coach down service to Pembroke Dock in July 1963. (M.J. Esau)

First published in Great Britain in 2022 by
Pen and Sword Transport
An imprint of
Pen & Sword Books Ltd.
Yorkshire - Philadelphia

ISBN 978 1 39909 572 3

Typeset in Palatino 11 / 13 by SJmagic DESIGN SERVICES, India.

Printed and bound in India by Replika Press Pvt. Ltd.

Pen & Sword Books Ltd incorporates the imprints of Pen & Sword Books Archaeology, Atlas, Aviation, Battleground, Discovery, Family History, History, Maritime, Military, Naval, Politics, Railways, Select, Transport, True Crime, Fiction, Frontline Books, Leo Cooper, Praetorian Press, Seaforth Publishing, Wharncliffe and White Owl.

For a complete list of Pen & Sword titles please contact

PEN & SWORD BOOKS LIMITED
47 Church Street, Barnsley, South Yorkshire, S70 2AS, England
E-mail: enquiries@pen-and-sword.co.uk
Website: www.pen-and-sword.co.uk

or

PEN AND SWORD BOOKS
1950 Lawrence Rd, Havertown, PA 19083, USA
E-mail: Uspen-and-sword@casematepublishers.com
Website: www.penandswordbooks.com

CONTENTS

DEDICATION

This volume is dedicated to the good people of Pembrokeshire who were fortunate enough to have their rail service between Whitland and Pembroke Dock retained under the Beeching cuts of 1964, and to the good people of Cardiganshire who lost their service between Whitland and Cardigan. Part of the reason why the Pembroke Dock branch survived must lie in the fact that the service served the resort town of Tenby which attracts much traffic to the line, whereas the branch to Cardigan has no intermediate locations of a similar significance. The earnings to the railway from passenger business on the Pembroke Dock branch must therefore have been much greater than on the Cardigan branch. Cardigan itself was however an important town with much agricultural traffic on the branch, and possibly in the present political climate it may have retained its rail service, notice being taken of the present interest in re-opening the Carmarthen to Aberystwyth line, which in some ways is comparable.

ACKNOWLEDGEMENTS

I am grateful to Pat Garland, Alan Wild and Mike Esau for use of their excellent steam age photographs in this book and to Stuart Warr and Stephen Miles for their diesel age material. Also to Tony Cooke for use of his excellent GWR Track Layouts for each station.

I have made every effort to identify all the copyright holders of pictorial and archive material used in this book. If I have wrongly attributed any material used, please email me at john_hodge@tiscali.co.uk if there is a need to rectify the position

PREFACE

We are now turning our attention away from the main line through from Carmarthen to Fishguard Harbour to the first of the retained main line branches from Whitland to Pembroke Dock, leaving only the branches to Milford Haven and Neyland to finish the series. We must however recognise the fact that the line from Clarbeston Road to Neyland was actually the main line before the opening of the line to Fishguard Harbour in 1906.

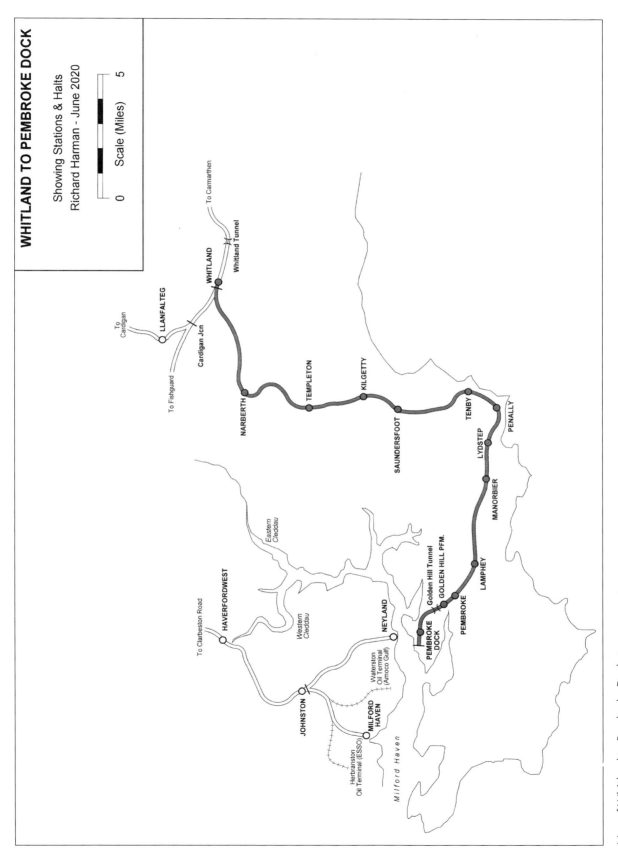

Map of Whitland to Pembroke Dock. (Richard Harman)

INTRODUCTION

In the early years of the century, an unnamed and unidentified Bulldog departs Pembroke Dock with a Class B service. The unnamed Bulldogs were all built between June and August 1906, so the date of the picture is later than that, but whether it is before or after the 28 December 1912 renumbering is not known.
(Author's Collection)

The western termini of the original South Wales Railway were planned to be at Fishguard and Pembroke Dock but were abandoned in favour of Neyland, with the town of Pembroke having to be satisfied with a ferry crossing of the River Cleddau from Neyland. This caused much discontent to the local inhabitants, who formed a company (the Pembroke and Tenby Railway, P&TR) in 1859 to make a railway from Pembroke Dock to Tenby with plans to extend this on to Narberth where it might meet up with a line to Central Wales. The plans did not conform with the South Wales Railway broad gauge as the planned line was to be narrow gauge which led to frosty relations between the two companies.

Though there was some difficulty in raising the capital for the building of the line, it was opened between Pembroke Town and Tenby in July 1863, and was extended back to Pembroke Dock the following year, when power was obtained from Parliament to extend their line through to Whitland, where it would meet up with the now Great Western line to/from Neyland and Carmarthen, a further 15¾ miles on from Tenby. Because of the gauge difference, the Pembroke & Tenby

Railway's station at Whitland would need to be separate from the Great Western, this being opened in September 1866.

This however did not satisfy the directors and they obtained further powers to extend their line another 15 miles to meet up with the Carmarthen & Cardigan Railway at Carmarthen, with the intention of linking up with the recently opened Llanelly Railway to gain access to the LNWR Central Wales line. These powers were however to be revoked if the GW would provide a narrow gauge line from Whitland to Carmarthen Bridge (over the River Towy). Not wanting to allow the LNWR access to West Wales by running powers over such a line, the GW agreed to convert their up line between Whitland and Carmarthen bridge into narrow gauge and to operate their broad gauge service over the down line. This thus became the first section of narrow gauge railway on the Great Western. This left the P&TR to make the connection with the GW line at Whitland and to construct a new narrow gauge line from Carmarthen Bridge to join with the Carmarthen & Cardigan line, the line being opened for goods in June 1868 and for passengers in August 1869. By this time, the Central Wales line had already been opened to Llandovery and the LNWR soon began working through coaches to the resort station of Tenby, no doubt causing much annoyance to the GW.

The Broad Gauge was abandoned in South and West Wales in May 1872 and from this time the P&TR ceased to run beyond Whitland and attached their vehicles to GW trains as far as Carmarthen Junction (then the station for Carmarthen), where they were detached and attached to Carmarthen & Cardigan trains. The loop which the P&TR had built into the C&C station at Carmarthen was demoted to a siding but when the new Carmarthen station was built

by the GW in 1902 it became part of a new triangle at Carmarthen Bridge.

At Pembroke Dock, a rail extension was constructed into the Dockyard for Admiralty use in 1871, first worked by the P&TR but taken over by the Admiralty in 1871, and also one to Hobbs Point in 1872, both being for goods traffic only.

The Whitland to Pembroke line as constructed was single throughout, with passing points at each main station. There are some steep gradients of 1 in 47-52, especially between Tenby and Whitland but trains are mostly light, of two or three coaches, except those which run through beyond Whitland, which need assistance for part of the journey.

An engine shed was provided at Whitland which allowed the working on the branch to be partly self-contained, and enabled power to also be provided for the Cardigan branch. Small sheds were also provided at Tenby and Pembroke Dock, the installation at Tenby reflecting its original importance.

Whitland suffered considerably as a railhead for the area under the closure of the Cardigan branch under the Beeching cuts of 1964. Much wagon load and part trainload traffic was lost following the cessation of wagonload traffic in 1976 in animal feedstuffs and fertiliser to individual stations, though this has been partly recouped with a new facility at Carmarthen.

With the advent of the diesel age, the shed was closed, with the line being operated by DMUs working through from Swansea and Carmarthen. All station sidings and connections have now been removed and the line is now single throughout, except at Tenby.

This train between Pembroke Dock and Pembroke Town is said to be a military special which may account for it being photographed. The motive power appears to be a 1076 Class pilot and a Dean Goods train engine. (Author's Collection)

At the same location as the previous picture, a 633 Class 0-6-0T '644' heads a period stopper bound for Pembroke Dock. 644 is confirmed as being a Whitland engine in the first decade of the new century. (Author's Collection)

LOCATION ANALYSIS

WHITLAND

Other than in the size of the sidings west of the station, the general appearance of Whitland station changed little from the first drawing available for 1875 to the final one for 1981.

The original Pembroke and Tenby Railway station at Whitland, closed in August 1869, was south of the South Wales Railway, and then the GWR line, in the area later occupied by the engine shed. The P&TR station, which was a dead end consisting of just one platform, probably had two sidings to its north and one to the south, together with an engine shed further to the south.

The GWR station in 1875 consisted of two island platforms, the main lines running between with bays on the north and south faces of each island. A goods shed was located centrally south of the down platform with two or three sidings to its south, which merged with the P&TR sidings, making it difficult to know which were P&TR and which SWR/GWR. A footbridge was provided at the east end of the station (still in place today) with Whitland East SB on the up side just beyond. Whitland West SB stood at the other end of the station on the up side, controlling the access to and from the Pembroke Dock line. There was one long siding north of the up main line.

Alterations to layout took place in 1877 when the down platform was lengthened, two additional sidings provided on the up side and an additional connection into the engine shed to keep clear of main lines.

By 1910, the siding accommodation west of the station on the north side of the up main line had been increased, the original siding being lengthened and two new long sidings and one short laid in parallel. On the down side, two new carriage sidings and a Ground Frame to control access to the down main had been provided by June 1900, the up side alterations taking place by August 1910.

East of the station, a private siding agreement operated by United Dairies began in June 1930, the physical works taking place in August of that year, but the siding did not apparently become operational until 1934.

By 1950, an Engineer's Pre-Assembly Depot had been created on the down side west of the station, consisting of four sidings, south of which a new engine turntable was provided in August 1950.

The engine shed closed to steam on 9 September 1963 and closed completely in January 1966.

The Down Siding east of the station was taken over by the Regent Oil Company on 1 November 1965, with a sole use of the siding and loading dock, but the agreement was terminated on 1 August 1968.

2 September 1972 was a landmark day at Whitland as the East and West SBs closed on that day and a new box opened on the down side at the east end of the station. The down siding east of the station was taken out of use, the Down Bay (Platform 1) became an Up and Down Bay, and the sidings forming the original Pembroke & Tenby Yard were removed. Further reductions to layout were made in March 1980 so that by 1981, the overall layout was similar to what it had been in 1875, without the P&T element, dictated by the needs of a passenger railway only.

A 45XX approaches the signal controlling entrance into Whitland station off the Pembroke Dock line with the signal for Platform 4 off on 24 May 1963. (P.J. Garland/Roger Carpenter)

A close-up view of the approach to Platform 4 with a full length train standing at Platform 3 and C and T indicators controlling the down main platform line on 24 May 1963. (P.J. Garland/Roger Carpenter)

A view of a rather deserted Whitland station in 1955 with a 45XX on a departure to either Cardigan or Pembroke Dock waiting at Platform 1, while on the up platform the station nameboard shows clearly "WHITLAND Junction For PEMBROKE AND TENBY and CARDIGAN". The Level Crossing can be seen at the end of the platforms at the east end of the station. Several examples of the barrow type then in use on all ex-GW stations can be seen. (Lens of Sutton)

The main line beyond Whitland station with the branch to Pembroke Dock going off to the right. The sidings alongside the main line show that Whitland was an important freight as well as passenger centre. (P.J. Garland/Roger Carpenter)

The controlling signal off the Pembroke Dock branch with the main arm with distant attached in the centre for Platform 3, the left arm for Platform 4 and the small siding signal for access to the engine shed which a 45XX has just taken on 24 May 1963. (P.J. Garland/Roger Carpenter)

The Pembroke Dock portion of a down London service is taken forward by 4575 Class No. 5571 as platform staff work the front van on the train for parcels and mail traffic on 26 June 1963. (C.M. & J.M. Bentley)

The above three coach train takes the Pembroke Dock line out of Whitland on 26 June 1963.
(C.M. & J.M. Bentley)

A Pembroke Dock portion of a down London service departs Whitland on 26 June 1963 with an insulated van next to engine 5545.
(C.M. & J.M. Bentley)

2251 Class No. 2287 at Platform 2 with the through four coach 12.25pm Shrewsbury to Pembroke Dock service via the Heart of Wales line which this engine would work through from Carmarthen on 7 September 1963. (W.G. Sumner)

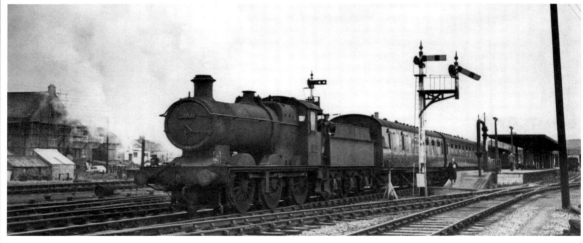

Another view of the 12.25pm Shrewsbury to Pembroke Dock four coach service leaving Whitland on the single line on 7 July 1962 with Carmarthen's 3214 in charge. (Alan Wild)

The 8.55am ex-Paddington has now become a stopping service for its three coach portion to Pembroke Dock, which is seen standing at the west end of Platform 2 and leaving the station on 31 August 1962 with 61XX No. 6114 in charge. (W.G. Sumner)

Another shot of the Pembroke Dock portion of the 8.55am ex-Paddington, this time on 31 May 1961, with Whitland based 2-6-2T No. 4107 in charge for the final leg of its journey. (L.R. Freeman/ Transport Treasury)

Three shots of
the 2pm Tenby to
Whitland with 45XX
2-6-2T No. 4557,
the first arriving at
Platform 4 on 31
August 1962, the
second a close-up
of the train engine
and the third
propelling the
stock back out of
the platform to the
down sidings.
(W.G. Sumner)

5571 with the 3.55pm from Pembroke Dock approaching Whitland with some fine Pembrokeshire scenery in the background on 7 July 1962. (Alan Wild)

A garish colour display at Whitland is provided by Class 153 single car 153303 (front) and Class 150 150279 (rear) on the 12.16 Pembroke Dock to Swansea service on 6 September 2003. (Stuart Warr)

Below left: The Summer Saturday 10.01 Pembroke Dock to Paddington HST service crosses from the branch to the main line at Whitland on 2 July 2013. (Stuart Warr)

Below right: The signalman at Whitland collects the token from the driver of this HST on the 14.55 Pembroke Dock to Paddington on 23 June 2018. (Stuart Warr)

Above: Highlight of the year for motive power enthusiasts was the visit of preserved King 6024 *King Edward I* to the Pembroke Dock branch on 1 May 2011. The return train is seen negotiating the crossover from the branch to the main line at Whitland. (Stuart Warr)

Below: As is usual for steam specials to West Wales, the down train was hauled from Carmarthen by a diesel engine, in this case Class 66 66192, seen trailing on the return journey. (Stuart Warr)

Above left: The Whitland to Tenby token is passed to the driver of the 11.05 Swansea to Pembroke Dock DMU by the Whitland East signalman as the train passes the now closed milk depot on 11 August 1990. (Stephen Miles)

Above right: The bracket signal controlling the junction at Whitland from the Pembroke Dock line as seen from the 16.38 Tenby to Swansea ECS off the 07.52 Leeds to Tenby on 11 August 1990. (Stephen Miles)

Below: Four cars form the 11.02 SO Pembroke Dock to Cardiff and Crewe which will split at Llanelli, the Crewe portion running via the Central Wales line, seen here running across the connection into the up main line at Whitland on 11 August 1990. (Stephen Miles)

Whitland
Engineering Yard
on 11 August 1990.
(Stephen Miles)

Whitland West End
as seen on 20 August
1987. (Jeff Stone)

5030 *Shirburn
Castle* approaching
Whitland with the
10.05 Cardiff to
Neyland Parcels on
17 May 1962.
(A. Cooke/Colour Rail)

The up Pembroke Coast Express 1.5pm Pembroke Dock to Paddington calls at Whitland with Manor 7825 *Lechlade Manor* in charge on 8 May 1963. (Colour Rail)

WHITLAND ENGINE SHED

The original shed at Whitland was opened by the Pembroke & Tenby Railway in 1863. The GWR absorbed the P&TR in 1897 and closed the shed in 1901. A replacement shed was brought from Letterston, which was actually a carriage shed displaced as an engine shed in 1895. In 1901, the GWR dismantled the carriage shed and transported it to Whitland where it became a one-road engine shed. The GWR improved the facility and later rebuilt it with a gable roof and this lasted throughout the steam era as Whitland shed, eventually closing in September 1963.

In practical terms, Whitland was a sub-shed of Neyland, though it had a fixed allocation of its own. Until 1961, Whitland housed mainly tank engines for the Pembroke Dock and Cardigan branch services and shunting engines for local shunting, though the 1901 allocation shows a Standard Goods 0-6-0 allocated. However, the final years of the depot saw an allocation of firstly a 43XX 2-6-0 in January 1961, soon replaced by Manor No. 7804 which was replaced later that year by No. 7825 which remained at the depot to supplement, even if only on a small scale, the tank engine fleet for the Pembroke Dock branch. The closure of the Cardigan branch to passenger services in September 1962 and to freight in May 1963, removed a large slice of the raison d'être for the depot, as the Pembroke Dock service could easily be operated from Carmarthen and the shed closed shortly afterwards in September 1963.

In 1901, the first year for which GWR allocation records are available, there were nine engines allocated, all saddle tanks except for one Standard Goods, as follows:-

Standard Goods 0-6-0 1 708
633 Class 0-6-0ST 2 639, 640
1016 Class 0-6-0ST 1 1032
1076 Buffalo 0-6-0ST 2 750, 1232
850 Class 0-6-0ST 2 1982, 2002
517 Class 0-4-2T 1 1158
Total 9

In addition, there were four engines allocated to Pembroke Dock which would have worked most days to Whitland and may well have needed maintenance there. These were two 'Stella' Class 2-4-0 (Nos. 3204 and 3506) and two 1854 Class 0-6-0ST (Nos. 1796 and 1858).

1910

By the start of 1910, the Whitland allocation remained at nine engines, but now six of them were of the 850 Class, obviously a popular engine for the depot's needs. The Standard Goods had gone and the other two residents were a 1076 and an 1813.

> 850 Class 0-6-0ST 861, 871, 1935, 1969, 1971, 1974
> 1076 Class 0-6-0ST 740
> 1813 Class 0-6-0ST 1844

There were now two engines recorded as based at Tenby, both 1076s (1255/85) and the Stella 2-4-0 (3506) was still at Pembroke Dock.

1920

By 1920, the number of engines allocated to Whitland had increased to fifteen. Of these, eight were of the 850 Class, one of the 645 Class, three of the 1076 Buffalo Class and two of the Dean Goods 2301 Class:-

> 850 Class 0-6-0ST and PT 851, 860, 861, 871, 872, 1952, 1957, 1986
> 645 Class 0-6-0ST and PT 653
> 1076 Class 0-6-0ST 1134, 1142, 1658
> 2301 Class 0-6-0 2364, 2539

A Buffalo 'No. 755' was shown as allocated to Tenby as was Steam Rail Motor No. 83. The experimental 4-4-2T No. 4600 was allocated to Pembroke Dock. Introduced in 1913, it was designed for the Birmingham local service as a successor to the Metro 2-4-0T, but this developed into a need for a larger engine (i.e. the 5101 Class 2-6-2T) and 4600 was transferred to work on the Whitland-Pembroke Dock line, shown actually allocated to Pembroke Dock between 1918 and 1925 when it was withdrawn, though this was eight years before the first of the 4500 Class 2-6-2Ts were allocated to Whitland, to which 4600 bore a marked resemblance.

1930

By 1930, the number of engines shown allocated to Whitland had fallen to ten, but the number shown working at Tenby and Pembroke Dock had risen to five. Three of the large 5101 Class 2-6-2Ts were now shown working from Pembroke Dock, Tenby and Whitland during the year, and these would doubtless all have really been based at Whitland for main exams. The

A scene at Whitland shed in the 1920s with 850 Class 0-6-0Ts 2010 and 1907 with 2301 Class 0-6-0s also present. (Lens of Sutton)

large 2-6-2Ts had arrived in the area but not as yet the smaller 45XXs.

2301 Class 0-6-0 2557
1016 Class 0-6-0PT 1071
850 Class 0-6-0PT 1219, 1221, 1941, 1942, 1948, 1975
1813 Class 0-6-0PT 1826
517 Class 0-4-2T 548

The following were shown as working at Tenby/Pembroke Dock/Whitland:-

2301 Class 0-6-0 2533
5101 Class 2-6-2T 5112, 5128, 5159
1076 Class 0-6-0ST 1590

In 1933, the 4500 Class was first tried at Whitland and this was the start of a very long association with the depot.

1940

By 1940, the Whitland allocation was at seventeen, over half of which were the 4500 Class 2-6-2T which had obviously been found well suited to working the Pembroke Dock and Cardigan services. There were still five of the old 850 Class 0-6-0Ts which were still well suited to their workload.

2251 Class 0-6-0 2288
2301 Class 0-6-0 2530
4500 Class 2-6-2T 4515, 4519, 4553, 4556, 4576, 4579, 5513, 5549, 5568
850 Class 0-6-0T 1964, 1979, 1996, 2010, 2018
5700 Class 0-6-0T 3637
Total 17

1950

By 1950, there had been several interesting changes at the depot where the passenger work on the Pembroke Dock and Cardigan branches had become dominated by the 4500 Class. These had now been joined for the Pembroke Dock line by a 5101 Class and an 8100 Class, a second example of which would soon arrive. The veteran 850 Class panniers remained at five but one of the new 1600 Class small panniers had

arrived at the depot, a class which would replace the 850s in the next few years. Also one of the 7400 Class had arrived from Fishguard, but this much-in-demand class would soon be concentrated on Carmarthen for branch working.

5101 Class 2-6-2T 4132
8100 Class 2-6-2T 8107
4500 Class 2-6-2T 4506, 4515, 4519, 4553, 4556, 4576, 4579, 5513, 5549, 5568
2251 Class 0-6-0 2288
7400 Class 0-6-0PT 7413
850 Class 0-6-0PT 1964, 1979, 1996, 2011, 2013
Total 19

During the year 1950, a second 81XX would arrive ex-Wolverhampton Works ...which was... 8102, as would a new 16XX No. 1628 in September.

1960

By 1960, all the oldest of the small Prairie 45XXs had been withdrawn while the whole of the 850 Class was now obsolete, replaced by the new 1600 Class Panniers. There were still ten of the newer 45 and 55XXs but these would soon be partly replaced on the Pembroke Dock services by the larger Prairies, especially the 61XXs allocated from the London Division, which replaced the 81XXs in West Wales, the whole class being withdrawn by 1965, with half based at Worcester. The detailed position at January 1960 was as follows:-

4300 Class 2-6-0 5357, 7320. 5357 survived a trip to Caerphilly Works in 2/60 and returned to Whitland.
5101 Class 2-6-2T 4122, 4132. 4107 was allocated from Landore in 6/60.
8100 Class 2-6-2T 8103, 8107. 8103 survived a trip to Swindon Works in 8/60 and was allocated to Carmarthen in 12/61.
4500 Class 2-6-2T 4550, 4556, 4557, 4558. 4550 was allocated to St.Blazey in 10/60 but immediately Condemned. 4556 was Condemned from Whitland in 6/60.

4575 Class 2-6-2T 4594, 5520, 5527, 5549, 5550, 5560. 4594 was Condemned in 11/60, 5527 in 6/60, 5560 transferred to Tondu in 6/60, and 5562 was allocated to Whitland in 6/60 but withdrawn in 7/60.

5700 Class 0-6-0PT 3657, 9714

Total 19 including 4107.

The 2251 Class 0-6-0 2288 had been put into Store in September 1959 and transferred to St Philips Marsh in November, ending Whitland's association with the class though examples from Carmarthen and Neyland continued to work through. The main event of the early 1960s was the arrival at Whitland of 61XXs, either direct from the London Division or having been first allocated to another South Wales depot. 6108 was allocated from Radyr in September 1960, 6148 from Didcot in the same month but went to Taunton in July 1961, 6114 from Landore in June 1961 and 6125 from Severn Tunnel in the July, returning to Old Oak Common in May 1962. The arrival of the 61XXs saw the removal of the 81XXs, half of the class ending their days at Worcester. An interesting arrival ex-Caerphilly Works in June 1960 was 6627, which joined the mixed traffic fleet.

Whitland Shed closed on 9 September 1963, when passenger services were covered by DMUs from Swansea and freights by Class 37 1,750HP. Brush 2,750 HP Diesel Electrics worked in on Summer Saturday long distance services from Leeds and York to Tenby while HSTs appeared on Summer Saturday trains from Paddington to Pembroke Dock still running as the Pembroke Coast Express. The new IET units have been approved for working similar trains through to Pembroke Dock.

A view of the single road shed itself with Whitland based 5549 standing outside and a 2251 in the yard. (John Hodge)

A variety of prairie tanks in front of the shed with 8107, a 4500 Class and a 4575 Class '5560' on the right. (G.W. Sharpe)

Originally Whitland had a large allocation of 850 Class 0-6-0ST and PT for the branches to Pembroke Dock and Cardigan. These were gradually replaced by newer engines but 2010 lasted until the early 1950s and is seen on the shed in 1950. (T.J. Edgington)

The 41XXs were one of the mainstays of the passenger working on the Pembroke Dock services. Here 4132 stands with 4122, both in work-stained condition, in the shed with the ubiquitous pannier early in the 1960s. (SLS)

A view of the shed yard from the field behind showing from l. to r. a 45XX, an 850, a 2301 and two more 45XXs on 31 May 1936. At this date, Whitland had an allocation of three 2301s (2409/40, 2544), so this was probably one of that trio. (SLS)

Another 1950 shot of an 850 Class at Whitland is this view of 1996 at the shed on 31 August 1950. It left Whitland for Duffryn Yard in November 1950, then moved to Neath and finally Gloucester in May 1951 from where it was withdrawn in January 1953.
(A. Delicata/R.K. Blencowe Collection)

The sort of group that was usually only available on shed on Sundays with 8739, 6114, 1645, 5520, 1666 and 1613, seen on Sunday 9 September 1962.
(Gavin Morrison)

There was always much interest in the 8100 Class as this was one of the few areas where several of the class were allocated. By 1956, there were four of the 8100 Class smaller wheeled 2-6-2Ts working in the Swansea District, Nos. 8102/7 at Whitland, 8103 at Carmarthen and 8104 at Neath. Here No. 8102 stands in the yard at Whitland shed with a 16XX on 5 April 1956. (John Hodge)

Another of the 81XX Class '8103' at Whitland shed on 17 May 1962. (A.Cooke/Colour Rail)

Recently ex-works (probably Caerphilly) 8107 in the yard with a 4575 Class on 10 May 1958. (Merchant Navy Locomotive Preservation Society)

The experimental 4-4-2T which was based at Pembroke Dock in its final years, lasting from November 1913 only until July 1925. (Manchester Locomotive Society)

It was common to find small groups of engines standing together in the yard as here with 16XX No. 1606 heading a quartet of Whitland based engines, made up of two panniers 'Nos. 8738/9' and a 4575 Class, No. 5550, against a stop block on 5 April 1956. (John Hodge)

1648 at Whitland shed on 6 July 1961. (L.W.Rowe/Colour Rail)

A close-up of 4575 Class No. 5550, a much-used engine on both the Pembroke Dock and Cardigan branches, on 5 April 1956. (John Hodge)

The large prairie tanks of the 5101 Class were very highly rated for the Pembroke Dock trains. 4131 was allocated to Whitland in the 1950s and is seen here on the depot. (D.K. Jones Collection)

43XXs were not uncommon visitors to the shed. Standing with 4575 Class No. 4579 is a 2-6-0 probably based at Neyland which has found itself possibly on loan to Whitland shed on 9 May 1953. (T.J. Edgington)

A group of engines on the coaling road which was carried out direct from wagons placed under the awning. No. 1613 and 5673 awaiting attention on 24 May 1963. A few examples of the 5600 Class were at Pembroke. (P.J. Garland/ Roger Carpenter)

Two large Prairie tanks '4132 and 5180' on shed at Whitland. (Colour Rail)

A view of the shed and coaling area on 26 June 1963 with Nos. 5571 and 6118 on the shed roads and a 4575 on the coaling road. (C.M. & J.M. Bentley)

No. 6118 standing at the entrance to the one road covered shed on 26 June 1963. The large pipes on the bogie bolsters alongside are for use in the building of the Texaco Pwllcrochan oil refinery opened in 1964 in the area. (C.M. & J.M. Bentley)

The 2251 Class 0-6-0s were a useful addition to the depot with No. 2288 seen here on shed with No. 1601 and just allocated No. 5673 on 4 May 1952. (Kidderminster Railway Museum)

An unusual engine to be working from Whitland in July 1962 was Llanelly's 4200 Class No. 4250 which was used on various trains on the Pembroke Dock branch during that month, the engine being withdrawn shortly after. It is here seen on shed on 7 July. (Alan Wild)

NARBERTH

Narberth is five miles west of Whitland, the station complex lying on a half circle curve with the platforms at the top. A diagram for 1899 shows two curved platforms of equal length with a signal box halfway along the up platform. Also on the up side was a goods yard with a goods shed and three other sidings for full load traffic. Cattle pens were available in a trailing siding on the down side east of the station. The up sidings were connected into the single line about ten chains east of the station to allow for train length. West of the station is Narberth Tunnel, 273 yards in length.

The cattle pens siding was taken out of use in December 1963 after BR ceased to carry cattle. The goods shed was closed and the siding serving it disconnected in July 1965 and the remaining sidings were taken out of use in October 1965. At this time, the down platform line was also taken out of use and single line working using the up platform initiated, when the signal box was also closed.

Narberth station looking east towards Whitland on 22 May 1963. The yard and goods shed are seen on the left. (P.J. Garland/ Roger Carpenter)

The view looking east on the same date from further down the platform, showing the main station buildings on the up platform and just a waiting shelter on the down. (P.J. Garland/Roger Carpenter)

The view westwards from Narberth station with the down starting signal and start of the single line running west to be seen on 22 May 1963. (P.J. Garland/Roger Carpenter)

The west end of the 273 yard tunnel showing the curve of the track on 22 May 1963. (P.J. Garland/Roger Carpenter)

The Pembroke Dock portion of the 11.55am from Paddington runs into Narberth on 9 August 1963 behind No. 4132 of Carmarthen. Wagons can be seen standing in the goods yard on the upper left. (Gerald Robinson)

Above left: Coming off the single line west of Narberth station, No. 5520 pilots No. 7320 on an up service on 12 September 1959. (F.K. Davies)

Above right: An up goods headed by 7 Vanfits behind 8750 Class No. 9748 runs into Narberth up platform in July 1963. (M.J. Esau)

Below: Running past Narberth's home signal on the single line is 4575 Class 2-6-2T No. 5545 on a down stopping service from Whitland to Pembroke Dock in July 1963. (M.J. Esau)

Approaching Narberth from Whitland, Manor No. 7814 *Fringford Manor* of Carmarthen heads the down Pembroke Coast Express in July 1963. (M.J. Esau)

Between Narberth and Templeton with the Prescelly Mountains in the background, No. 4135 heads a down stopping service to Pembroke Dock in July 1963. (M.J. Esau)

Local pannier No. 9748 heads a down goods between Narberth and Templeton in July 1963. (M.J. Esau)

A view ahead into Narberth station from a train hauled by Manor No. 7804 *Baydon Manor* on 26 April 1961, as an up goods waits in the platform for line clear onto the single line to Whitland.
(C.M. & J.M. Bentley)

Manor No. 7804 waits at the down platform with a Whitland to Pembroke Dock train on 26 April 1961.
(C.M. & J.M. Bentley)

A close-up view of the up platform's station buildings from the east end on 20 June 1962 as a down freight passes on the other platform line.
(R.G. Nelson/Terry Walsh)

The up Pembroke Coast Express waits at the up platform behind Carmarthen Manor No. 7814 *Fringford Manor* on 20 July 1963, two months before the cessation of portion working on London services to West Wales. (W.G. Sumner)

The up Pembroke Coast Express pulls out of Narberth behind Carmarthen Manor No. 7814 *Fringford Manor* on 20 July 1963. (W.G. Sumner)

A rear view of the same train at the start of the single line towards Whitland. The headboard on the coaches was PADDINGTON TENBY PEMBROKE DOCK. (W.G. Sumner)

Above: Small and large prairie tanks No. 5571 and 4136 double head the 7.5am Derby to Pembroke Dock via the Central Wales line into Narberth on 20 July 1963. (W.G. Sumner)

Right: The same pair head west out of Narberth towards the entrance to the tunnel. (W.G. Sumner)

Below: The down Pembroke Coast Express stands at the down platform behind Carmarthen Manor No. 7804 *Baydon Manor* on 7 September 1963 on the last day of through working between Paddington and West Wales, after which all London services terminated and started from Swansea and passengers changed at Swansea into a DMU to go forward. (W.G. Sumner)

A full view of
Narberth station
looking east from
the end of the
down platform on
31 August 1962.
(W.G. Sumner)

The 3.50pm
Pembroke Dock
to Whitland local
service behind
No. 5545 running
bunker-first waits at
the up platform on
7 September 1963.
(W.G. Sumner)

A distant view
of the 12.55pm
Whitland to Tenby
approaching
Narberth showing
the cattle pens and
wagons in the goods
yard on 31 August
1962. (W.G. Sumner)

The same train running into the platform at Narberth. (W.G. Sumner)

The same train standing at the down platform. The fireman would be stoking up the fire for the climb to Templeton. (W.G. Sumner)

42xx No. 4250 running into Narberth with a freight from Pembroke Dock on 7 July 1962. (Alan Wild)

An HST at Narberth. Power Car 43042 heads the 08.12 Paddington to Pembroke Dock Summer Saturday working on 23 June 2018. (Stuart Warr)

Cold Blow summit at Narberth is the location of this excellent shot of the latest Class 800 IET as it works the GWR 08.45 Paddington to Pembroke Dock Summer Saturday 1B15 Pembroke Coast Express on 8 June 2019, hopefully setting the scene for the future deployment of these trains on this route in summer. (Stephen Miles)

TEMPLETON

Templeton is located just over three miles west of Narberth and until 1906 was on a single line, with a signal box, closed in 1897, towards the east end of the platform and a single siding beyond the station on the up side equipped with cattle pens.

The station appears to have been closed in 1897 but re-opened on 1 May 1906 with new facilities. A new signal box had opened in October 1905 at the west end of the single platform and a new down/up loop was provided with spurs at either end, capable of holding a train length. A siding was laid in south of the loop with a spur at the west end.

On 1 February 1915, a down platform was brought into use and the station became a passing point on the otherwise single line, the down platform line being the original down/up loop. The down

siding was still provided, the spur at the west end being replaced by trap points in 1927. The up siding was taken out of use in November 1963. The station was closed in 1965 and reverted to a single line as from 1 October that year, the signal box being closed on 3 October.

A saddle tank stands at the head of a down goods at the west end of Templeton platform in this posed picture early in the twentieth century. (Lens of Sutton)

A view of Templeton looking east from the west end of the platforms on 21 May 1963. (P.J. Garland/ Roger Carpenter)

A view of Templeton looking east showing the signal box and down siding with loading gauge on 22 May 1963.
(P.J. Garland/Roger Carpenter)

Templeton looking west from the end of the down platform on 22 May 1963.
(P.J. Garland/Roger Carpenter)

Pulling out of Templeton, No. 2287 heads the 12.54pm Whitland to Tenby local on 9 August 1963. The up siding west of the signal box has an empty mineral wagon standing ready for collection.
(Gerald T. Robinson)

4575 Class No. 5571 comes off the 7.5am Derby to Pembroke Dock which it has assisted from Whitland and runs along the up main on 20 July 1963. (W.G. Sumner)

The 7.5am Derby to Pembroke Dock pulls away from Templeton behind No. 4136 with No. 5571, which has assisted the train from Whitland, standing outside the signal box on 20 July 1963. (W.G. Sumner)

The same train heading away west. (W.G. Sumner)

Above: Whitland's 5600 Class No. 5673 with the 7.55am Paddington to Pembroke Dock at Templeton on 20 July 1963. The wagons in the down siding contain heavy pipework for the Texaco Pwllcrochan Oil Refinery, then being constructed. (W.G. Sumner)

Below: No. 4557 with the two coach 2pm Tenby to Whitland stands at Templeton up platform on 31 August 1962. (W.G. Sumner)

Manor No. 7814 *Fringford Manor* pulls away from Templeton with a down local stopping train in July 1963. (M.J. Esau)

Manor No. 7826 *Longworth Manor* near Templeton with a down stopping service in July 1963. (M.J. Esau)

KILGETTY

Kilgetty lies 2½ miles west of Templeton on the single line. The platform was originally on the up side of the line but by 1895 had been moved to the down side. There was a signal box towards the west end of the platform on the 1895 plan but this closed in 1897. West of the station was a trailing connection (worked from a ground frame) into a small down side yard consisting of one long siding split into two towards the east end, to provide cattle pens. The sidings were all removed in June 1965.

Kilgetty single line platform looking east on 8 July 1958.
(R.M. Casserley)

Kilgetty looking west on 31 August 1962.
(W.G. Sumner)

The 10.55am from Paddington, Pembroke Coast Express, four coaches west of Swansea stands at the down platform at Kilgetty on 8 July 1958.
(R.M. Casserley)

Kilgetty Goods Yard seen from a Whitland bound train on 24 May 1963. (P.J. Garland/Roger Carpenter)

The 12.55pm Whitland to Tenby calls at Kilgetty with 4500 Class 2-6-2T No. 4569 in charge on 22 August 1962. The canted track is visible in the second image. (Gerald T. Robinson)

The 2pm Tenby to Whitland at Kilgetty with engine No. 4557 on 31 August 1962. (W.G. Sumner)

Kilgetty looking east with the Templeton distant signal near the connection into the goods yard.
(P.J. Garland/Roger Carpenter)

Manor No. 7814 *Fringford Manor* between Templeton and Kilgetty with a four coach down service to Pembroke Dock in July 1963.
(M.J. Esau)

Whitland's No. 5545 approaching Kilgetty with a down service in July 1963. (M.J. Esau)

Whitland's No. 4136 with a down goods approaching Kilgetty on the single line in July 1963. (M.J. Esau)

SAUNDERSFOOT

The present Saundersfoot station is located less than a mile west of Kilgetty, but was originally three quarters of a mile further west, near a connection to Moreton Colliery, closed in 1887.

Saundersfoot was originally a place of considerable importance with its own 4ft. gauge Saundersfoot Railway opened in 1829. The first line to be constructed connected Stepaside/Kilgetty Collieries with Saundersfoot Harbour running along the coast through a series of short tunnels and through the centre of the town. The second line ran between Reynalton Colliery 'north of the future main line' and Saundersfoot Harbour with an incline of 1 in 5 some half a mile from the harbour, well south of the future main line. The line crossed the main line through a tunnel under the main line, the new Raynalton Anthracite Colliery's PSA dated 17 October 1914. The Saundersfoot Railway was the first railway line in Pembrokeshire and remained independent until closure in 1939.

About half a mile west of the station was a connection out of the single line south to Bonvilles Court Colliery, opened in 1840, which was a substantial complex of sidings again leading to Saundersfoot Harbour and also worked by the Saundersfoot Railway.

A plan for 1907 shows the station consisting of two platforms with a signal box towards the east end of the down platform and was a passing point on the otherwise single line. East of the station on the down line, there was a facing connection into a yard, which became a location for Camping Coaches. The single siding connection split into three sidings at the west end of the platforms. The siding nearest the running lines was removed pre-1960 but the others were taken out of use in January 1965, and the signal box and up platform line in October 1965. This left only the down platform, served by a single line which now became bi-directional.

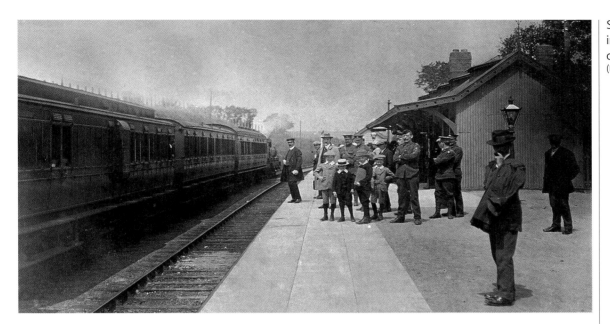

Saundersfoot station in the early years of the century.
(Lens of Sutton)

The Saundersfoot Miners Express that ran through the streets conveying miners in the early years of the century.
(Lens of Sutton)

Saundersfoot, another passing place on the single line, looking east on 21 May 1963.
(P.J. Garland/Roger Carpenter)

Looking west with the down platform line running into the single line. (P.J. Garland/ Roger Carpenter)

A view of the main platform from an up train on 27 August 1959. (R.K. Blencowe Collection)

A view against the sun of the up Pembroke Coast Express leaving Saundersfoot on 22 August 1962 behind Carmarthen Manor No. 7829 *Ramsbury Manor*, showing the trailing connection into the goods yard. (Gerald T. Robinson)

Coming off the single line into the down platform, a Class 1 service hauled by two large prairie tanks, Nos. 4132 and 4122. And the same pair leaving to rejoin the single line. (D.K. Jones Collection)

An up service hauled by No. 4122 runs into the up platform in the 1950s.
(G.W. Sharpe Collection)

An up freight hauled by 43XX No. 7320 starts from the up platform after waiting for the road on 13 June 1959.
(D.K. Jones Collection)

An eastbound train of empty stock leaves Saundersfoot behind unusual power for the line in Llanelly's No. 7225 on 9 August 1963. The engine had possibly worked a special down freight for the building of Pwllcrochan Oil Refinery.
(Gerald T. Robinson)

Whitland's No. 5673 with the 7.55am ex-Paddington at Saundersfoot on 20 July 1963.
(W.G. Sumner)

Two views of
the goods yard
at Saundersfoot,
the second with a
Camping Coach on
a truncated piece of
track in May 1963.
(P.J. Garland/Roger Carpenter)

The 12.55pm from
Whitland to Tenby
makes its call at
Saundersfoot with
No. 4557 in charge
on 31 August 1962.
(W.G. Sumner)

Carmarthen Manor No. 7825 *Lechlade Manor* calls at Saundersfoot with the up Pembroke Coast Express, 1.5pm ex-Pembroke Dock to Paddington … and departs on 31 August 1962, all views mostly against the sun. (W.G. Sumner)

Saundersfoot station looking east on 31 August 1962. (W.G. Sumner)

The 8.55am ex-Paddington runs into Saundersfoot on 20 July 1963 behind 61XX No. 6118. During this period the WR were using several ex-LNER seconds as strengthening vehicles on London services, one of which is the front coach. (W.G. Sumner)

The Class 120 Cross Country DMUs were the basic workhorses for the Class B and many Class A services. Here a three car set is seen at Saundersfoot with a Whitland to Pembroke Dock service on 2 August 1980, when the station was in the course of rebuilding. (Stuart Warr)

TENBY

The original Pembroke & Tenby Railway had its station, engine shed and fitting shops south of the present location of Tenby station, the site accessed until 1965 via Black Rock Sidings Ground Frame, west of Tenby. The original passenger station closed on 4 September 1866 but became a wagon shops. The engine shed was moved from the north side of the complex to the south side to take over the former fitting shops and lasted until 1959, with one or two engines being allocated probably until the 1930s.

A plan for 1899 shows the new station in place at 274m. 53ch. with up and down platforms and an up Back Platform line with signal box located alongside at the west end of the platform. Cattle pens were provided in a short siding at the east end of the down platform. East of the station is the 148 yard Tenby Viaduct.

A plan for 1920 shows a goods yard complex with a goods shed south of the up platform, the back line having disappeared. The signal box closed in May 1956 and was replaced by a new structure at the west end of the down platform. The complex remained as such until the mass rationalisation of the area's trackwork in 1966, when all but the single main line and platforms crossing place were taken out of use, the connection at Black Rock Ground Frame to the original station and facilities having been taken out the year before.

Tenby station looking east towards Whitland on 21 May 1963. The down platform from Whitland was Platform 1 and the up No. 2. (P.J. Garland/ Roger Carpenter)

The view west from Tenby station with a train proceeding towards Pembroke Dock. The track on the right leads into the goods yard. (R.K. Blencowe Collection)

A view along the platforms looking west past the footbridge, the westbound platforms on the left and the eastbound on the right. (R.G.Nelson/Terry Walsh)

A view from the down platform looking across to the Goods Yard and Goods Shed, 27 August 1959. (R.K. Blencowe Collection)

A view from an access road on 24 May 1953 showing the signal box on the down side with 56XX No. 5673 on a down train and the goods yard on the up side. (P.J. Garland/Roger Carpenter)

Two views of Whitland's No. 5571 with the 2 coach (BSK and Compo) Pembroke Dock portion off the 11.55am ex-Paddington waiting at the down platform on 21 May 1963. (P.J. Garland/Roger Carpenter)

Whitland's 56XX No. 5603 with a down goods stands at the west end of the down platform on 12 August 1949. (F.K. Davies)

Above: Taking water at the east end of the up platform is Whitland's No. 4579 on 11 August 1949. (F.K. Davies)

Left: Carmarthen Manor No. 7829 *Ramsbury Manor* climbs away from Tenby towards Saundersfoot with the up Pembroke Coast Express on 9 August 1963. (Gerald T. Robinson)

Below: 5550 stands at the west end of the down platform with the 6.50pm Tenby to Pembroke Dock as the double-headed 6.15pm Pembroke Dock to Whitland arrives with 4132 piloting 5357 on 20 June 1957. (John Wiltshire)

A pair of Whitland Prairie tanks, 4132 and 8107, take water at the east end of the up platform with the 6.15pm Pembroke Dock to Whitland on 19 June 1957. (John Wiltshire)

5549 runs into the down platform with the Pembroke Dock portion of the 8.55am from Paddington on 18 June 1957. (John Wiltshire)

A down local service hauled by a 41XX leaving Tenby with the estuary in the background in July 1963. (M.J. Esau)

An up service from Pembroke Dock approaching Tenby on the single line, formed of local and main line stock with a parcel van between in July 1963. (M.J. Esau)

The view west from Tenby on 24 May 1963 showing the single line sweeping round to the right and the up home signal for Tenby box, the two arms referring to the up platform and Goods lines. (P.J. Garland/Roger Carpenter)

The ground frame controlling entry to Black Rock (Quarry) Sidings to the west of Tenby station on 24 May 1963. (P.J. Garland/Roger Carpenter)

The line going off west of Tenby station from the Black Rock Siding GF leading to the original station, lower yard and engine shed and Black Rock Quarries, as on 24 May 1963. The branch was taken out of use in July 1965. See text for details. (P.J. Garland/ Roger Carpenter)

Stone built overbridge west of Tenby on 24 May 1963. (P.J. Garland/Roger Carpenter)

A local service between Tenby and Penally behind Whitland's No. 5193 in August 1961. (Roger Carpenter Collection)

Carmarthen Manor No. 7825 *Lechlade Manor* starts away west from Tenby with a two coach local service in the early 1960s as seen from the approach road to the station.
(John Spencer Gilks)

Whitland's No. 5549 brings a short goods from Pembroke Dock into the goods sidings at Tenby in 1960.
(Roger Carpenter Collection)

56xx No. 6688 heads a 5 coach up service near Tenby on 4 August 1950.
(E.R. Morten)

Carmarthen Manor No. 7804 *Baydon Manor* at the down platform with a stopping train to Pembroke Dock on 26 April 1961, showing the goods depot on the up side to good advantage.
(C.M. & J.M. Bentley)

Two views of a 3 coach portion of a down London service waiting at Tenby, also conveying what appears to be a van of fish from Milford Haven via Whitland on 26 June 1963.
(C.M. & J.M. Bentley)

Whitland's No., 4557 waits at the down platform with the 12.55pm terminating train from Whitland as the up Pembroke Coast Express stands at the up platform on 31 August 1962. (W.G. Sumner)

A down freight hauled by Neyland's No. 7320 awaits the road beyond Tenby as an 8750 Class pannier shunts the goods yard in the early 1960s. (R.K. Blencowe Collection)

Not the August weather seaside holiday makers wanted at Tenby on 23 August 1962, as Carmarthen Manor No. 7825 *Lechlade Manor* runs in with the 3 coach 10.47am service from Whitland to Pembroke Dock. (Gerald T. Robinson)

The down Pembroke Coast Express with its Pembroke Dock portion strengthened by an additional SK runs into Tenby behind Carmarthen's Manor No. 7814 *Fringford Manor* on 20 July 1963 and stands in the down platform. (W.G. Sumner)

The 8.55am from Paddington had three coaches for Pembroke Dock plus an ER strengthening second front and are seen behind Whitland 61XX No. 6118 on 20 July 1963. (W.G. Sumner)

The 8.55am Paddington has its three coach Pembroke Dock portion strengthened by an MR second No. M3112M as it arrives and departs from Tenby behind Whitland's No. 4132 on 7 September 1963, the last day on which portion working to West Wales existed.
(W.G. Sumner)

Four views of the 3.50pm Pembroke Dock to Whitland behind Whitland's No. 5545 with three coaches and a van front and rear as it stands at and departs from Tenby on 20 July 1963.
(W.G. Sumner)

A steam special in May 1993 brought Black 5 44767 to Tenby seen here heading east at the down platform. (John Davies)

The up Pembroke Coast Express runs into Tenby behind Carmarthen Manor No. 7825 *Lechlade Manor* on 31 August 1962. (W.G. Sumner)

Whitland pannier No. 9748 brings empty bogie bolsters back from the building of the Texaco Oil Refinery ar Pwllcrochan on 20 July 1963. (W.G. Sumner)

The 7.5am Derby to Pembroke Dock stands at Tenby and then departs behind No. 6118 on 7 September 1963. (W.G. Sumner)

The exterior of Tenby station on 1 June 1961. (L.R. Freeman/ Transport Treasury)

Three views of 56XX No. 6680 arriving and standing at Tenby with the 10.45am Whitland to Pembroke Dock on 1 June 1961.
(L.R Freeman/Transport Treasury)

Tenby station showing footbridge looking east on 1 June 1961. (L.R. Freeman/Transport Treasury)

Carmarthen Manor No. 7804 *Baydon Manor* on the 9.50am Whitland to Pembroke Dock on 1 June 1961, the return working being the Up Pembroke Coast Express 1.10pm Pembroke Dock-Paddington. (L.R. Freeman/Transport Treasury)

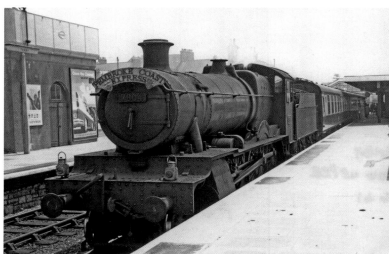

Whitland's No. 4122 taking water with the 11.55am Paddington three coach portion to Pembroke Dock plus a van of fish on 12 July 1962. The driver and fireman look on. (Alan Wild)

Long term Barry engine now allocated to Whitland No. 6627 brings the 6.15pm Pembroke Dock to Whitland into Tenby formed of three coaches and a returning empty fish van for Milford Haven on 12 July 1962. (Alan Wild)

An unusual engine to be working on the Pembroke Dock branch was this Llanelly 42XX No. 4250 which was on the line in July 1962 seen heading a westbound freight through Tenby. (Alan Wild)

The original engine shed at Tenby. (SLS)

The Class 47s were introduced in the mid-1960s and gradually became a general utility engine for main line passenger and freight. Here 47191 brings the ECS for the 09.15 Tenby to York (a relic of the Pembroke & Tenby Railway service concept) into Tenby on 2 August 1980. (Stuart Warr)

Having run round, the Class 47 reverses the stock back into the platform. (Stuart Warr)

In the livery current at that time, an HST runs into Tenby with the return 15.05 SO Pembroke Dock to Paddington summer service, running as the Pembroke Coast Express on 25 September 2004, the last day of that year's summer timetable. (Stuart Warr)

Two views of the Summer Saturday 08.45 Paddington to Pembroke Dock HST at Tenby, first running into the down arrival platform and then a rear view with the 13.09 Pembroke Dock to Swansea at the up platform on 20 July 2013. (Stuart Warr)

Above: September 1969 and Tenby is looking at its best in the Summer sun as a Class 120 departs for Pembroke Dock. (Peter Jones)

Below: HST Power Car 43002 leads the 09.40 SO Paddington to Pembroke Dock service into Tenby on 16 July 1988. (Stephen Miles)

The 09.30 Paddington to Pembroke Dock SO leaves Tenby towards Penally on 11 August 1990. (Stephen Miles)

Class 101 DMU S804 calls at Tenby with the 14.09 Swansea to Pembroke Dock service on 4 July 1987. (Stephen Miles)

Class 108 DMU S945 with the 11.15 Pembroke Dock to Swansea making the Tenby call on 4 July 1987. (Stephen Miles)

Three views of the
down platform
at Tenby in both
directions on
20 August 1987.
(Jeff Stone)

The 09.14 York to Tenby with 47547 returns to Swansea as the 17.35 service on 4 July 1987.
(Stephen Miles)

PENALLY

Penally is located just over a mile west of Tenby, with a single platform located on the single line. There was originally a signal box, the location of which is not known, but the box was closed in about 1897. The platform was extended eastwards in about 1904 to end at the level crossing at the east end of the complex. West of the station was a siding, authorised in 1904 and removed in 1965. This was operated from a ground frame 8ch. west of the platform.

Penally was a Camping Coach spot and two such coaches are seen in the siding on 21 May 1963.
(P.J. Garland/Roger Carpenter)

Four views of Penally single line platform, looking west and east. (P.J. Garland/Roger Carpenter, R.G.Nelson/Terry Walsh, Great Western Trust)

A Grange on the branch. No. 6804 *Brockington Grange* heads the 9.40am Swansea to Pembroke Dock near Penally on 9 August 1963. (Gerald T. Robinson)

The lovely Pembrokeshire countryside forms the backdrop for this view of No. 6804 returning from Pembroke Dock with the 4.50pm ECS to Tenby on 9 August 1963. (Gerald T. Robinson)

The four coach portion of the 10.55am ex-Paddington Pembroke Coast Express behind Carmarthen Manor No. 7804 *Baydon Manor* approaching Penally on 9 August 1963. (Gerald T. Robinson)

Above: The Pembroke Dock portion of the 8.55am from Paddington with an ER second on the front makes the Penally stop behind No. 6118 on 20 July 1963. (W.G. Sumner)

Below left: A view of Penally platform on 20 July 1963. (W.G. Sumner)

Below right: There were Manors in profusion on the line by July 1963 when No. 7814 *Fringford Manor* was recorded near Penally with a four coach local train. (M.J. Esau)

Whitland's No. 5545 makes the Penally call with the 3.50pm Pembroke Dock to Whitland on 20 July 1963. (W.G. Sumner)

No. 4569 approaching Penally with the Pembroke Dock portion of a train from London plus a fish van in August 1961. (Roger Carpenter Collection)

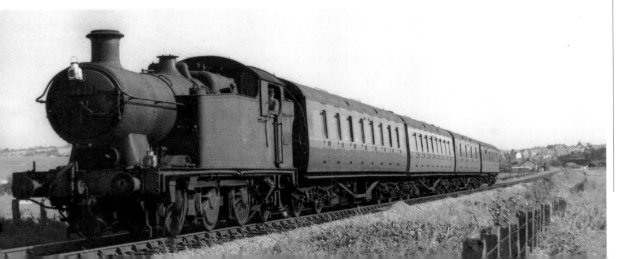

Whitland's No. 6623 with a four coach train to Pembroke Dock between Tenby and Penally in August 1961. (Roger Carpenter Collection)

Approaching Penally from Manorbier, No. 4132 in charge of the 10.20am Pembroke Dock to Paddington 7 coach portion on 7 July 1962. (Alan Wild)

No. 4107 at the same location with the 11.25am Pembroke Dock to Paddington, conveying a local set to Whitland on 7 July 1962. (Alan Wild)

Near Penally with the 10.45am Whitland to Pembroke Dock, Manor No. 7825 *Lechlade Manor* will be set to return with the up Pembroke Coast Express on 7 July 1962. (Alan Wild)

Possibly working on the line to help out with the increased freight traffic for the building of Pwllcrochan oil refinery. No. 4250 of Llanelly approaches Penally with a branch goods service on 7 July 1962.
(Alan Wild)

In modern times, the 13.05 Pembroke Dock to Swansea calls at Penally with Class 150 unit 150231 in charge.

(Stuart Warr)

LYDSTEP HALT

Lydstep Halt was located 1¾ miles west of Penally and was in use in 1899, though an official date of opening is given as 1905. It was closed in January 1956. As a halt, no passenger facilities were provided and notice had to be given to the guard by passengers wishing to alight, and a hand signal given by passengers on the platform to the driver if they wished to entrain.

Lydstep Halt on the single line looking west on 21 May 1963. No facilities were provided at this halt, and it was up to passengers to protect themselves in inclement weather. (P.J. Garland/ Roger Carpenter)

No. 5571 passing Lydstep on the 9.50am Whitland to Pembroke Dock on 21 May 1963. (P.J. Garland/Roger Carpenter)

No. 6118 passing Lydstep Halt with the 10.30am Pembroke Dock to Whitland on 21 May 1963. (P.J. Garland/Roger Carpenter)

Stone underbridge at Lydstep on 21 May 1963. (P.J. Garland/ Roger Carpenter)

MANORBIER

Manorbier was located 1½ miles west of Lydstep Halt. A drawing of the layout in c.1880 showed the station to consist of one platform on a single line with a level crossing at the east end, a loop line south of the running line and a short siding south of that.

In 1895, a down platform was added, utilising the loop line which was extended to allow the station to become a useful passing point. A signal box was opened in that year towards the west end of the up platform and a siding ran from the down line back behind the down platform.

In October 1965, the down line was taken out of use and single line working over the up line restored. The two sidings (increased from the previous one) behind the down platform were taken out of use and the signal box closed in the same year.

Manorbier double line passing point platforms looking east on 21 May 1963. (P.J. Garland/ Roger Carpenter)

A closer view of the level crossing looking east on 21 May 1963. (P.J. Garland/Roger Carpenter)

The diminutive Manorbier signal box on 21 May 1963. (P.J. Garland/Roger Carpenter)

The up platform at Manorbier looking east showing the small signal box and station buildings on 24 May 1963. (P.J. Garland/Roger Carpenter)

Two views of No. 5571 standing at Manorbier on the 9.50am Whitland to Pembroke Dock on 24 May 1963. (P.J. Garland/Roger Carpenter)

Mogul No. 7318 pilots 5560 on an up London service into Manorbier on 12 September 1959. (F.K. Davies)

No. 6118 near Manorbier working empty bogie bolsters back from the site of the new oil refinery at Pwllcrochan on 9 August 1963. (Gerald T. Robinson)

The up Pembroke Coast Express three coach portion leaves Manorbier behind Carmarthen Manor No. 7814 *Fringford Manor* in July 1963. (M.J. Esau)

A 41xx runs into Manorbier off the single line from Lamphey as a 45XX waits to depart with a down service in 1963. (John Spencer Gilks)

Manorbier station from the level crossing on 20 July 1963. (W.G. Sumner)

No. 7814 returns from Pembroke Dock in charge of the 1.5pm to Paddington, Pembroke Coast Express on 20 July 1963. (W.G. Sumner)

No. 4132 heads through the station with empty bogie bolsters from the Pwllcrochan oil refinery site on 20 July 1963. (W.G. Sumner)

No. 4159 runs into Manorbier with the 10.30am Pembroke Dock to Whitland on 1 June 1961 and takes water for the journey ahead. (L.R. Freeman/ Transport Treasury)

Looking along the platforms from the west end as Carmarthen Manor No. 7804 *Baydon Manor* calls with the 9.50am Whitland to Pembroke Dock on 1 June 1961.
(L.R. Freeman/ Transport Treasury)

Carmarthen Manor No. 7804 *Baydon Manor* at the down platform with the two coach 9.50am from Whitland on 1 June 1961.
(L.R. Freeman/ Transport Treasury)

56xx No. 6680 awaits time at Manorbier with the 10.45am Whitland to Pembroke Dock on 1 June 1961.
(L.R. Freeman/ Transport Treasury)

Above left: The usual Class 120 on this 08.44 Whitland to Pembroke Dock service passing through Manorbier. (Stuart Warr)

Above right and below: Power is now provided by Class 150 and 153 units as here with the 15.05 Pembroke Dock to Swansea formed with 153353 on 26 April 2011, also seen departing Manorbier over the LC. (Stuart Warr)

BEAVERS HILL HALT

Beavers Hill Halt was three quarters of a mile west of Manorbier and came into use in May 1905, with a level crossing operated by a ground frame at the east end. The crossing was left open from June 1965, covered by a W sign for the driver to sound the horn on passing trains.

About a mile further west was Manorbier Newton Level Crossing operated by a ground frame but this was also left open from June 1965.

Beavers Hill Halt looking west on the single line west of Manorbier on 21 May 1963.
(P.J. Garland/Roger Carpenter)

The level crossing at the east end of Beavers Hill Halt on 21 May 1963.
(P.J. Garland/Roger Carpenter)

Beavers Hill crossing after removal of the gates in June 1965.
(Stephenson Locomotive Society)

Beavers Hill Halt looking east.
(W.G. Sumner)

No. 5673 with a short down goods near Beavers Hill on 21 May 1963.
(P.J. Garland/Roger Carpenter)

LAMPHEY

Lamphey stands about three miles west of Beavers Hill Halt and consists of a single platform on the single line. There was originally a signal box on the east end of the platform, but this was closed in 1897. A level crossing was at the east end of the platform. A loop siding ran south of the single line controlled by a ground frame at both ends. This was removed in December 1963 and only the single running line was operative thereafter.

Lamphey station looking west seen from the overbridge at the east end of the station on 21 May 1963. Wagons in the siding are in connection with the building of Pwllcrochan oil refinery. (P.J. Garland/ Roger Carpenter)

A Steam Rail Motor calls at Lamphey with a 4-wheeler and a van attached in the early years of the century. (Author's Collection)

Two views of Lamphey station looking east along the single platform, the first on 20 July 1963, the second undated. (W.G. Sumner)

6118 at Lamphey with the 6.22pm Pembroke Dock to Whitland on 20 July 1963. (W.G. Sumner)

Manor No. 7814 *Fringford Manor* standing at and leaving Lamphey with the down Pembroke Coast Express on 20 July 1963. (W.G. Sumner)

6118 passes under the overbridge at the east end of Lamphey station and heads for Manorbier on 20 July 1963. (W.G. Sumner)

No. 2287 with the 11.55am Shrewsbury to Pembroke Dock via the Central Wales line approaching Lamphey on 20 July 1963. The engine had worked the up balancing service through to Llandeilo and had taken over the down train from there. (W.G. Sumner)

PEMBROKE

Pembroke is about one and a half miles west of Lamphey and almost two miles from Pembroke Dock. The station lies on a curve and a drawing for 1880 showed two goods sidings coming off a loop on the single line east of the station. By 1896, a third siding had been added with cattle pens and a signal box on the south side of the single line opened in 1895, 7 chains east of the station.

Sidings were laid in on the south side east of the signal box in about 1917 when the signal box was also renewed. A private siding for T.W. Colley & Sons was laid in on the up side off the northernmost siding in the yard with a PSA in February 1925, the agreement renewed in September 1936.

By 1955, a down loop had been added, giving loops on both sides of the single running line and there were two sidings to the south. The layout remained thus until 1971 when the downside loop and sidings on the south side were all taken out of use in September, when the signal box was also closed. The up sidings remained in use, but the private siding agreement had been terminated in 1968, the siding being removed in 1975.

Between Pembroke and Pembroke Dock, Golden Hill Platform existed half a mile west of Pembroke, having been opened on 1 July 1909 and closed on 5 February 1940. Half a mile beyond was the Golden Hill (or Pembroke) Tunnel, 460 yards long, on the single line to Pembroke Dock.

Pembroke single line platform looking east. The trolley load of milk churns is in keeping with the farming nature of the area. The stone building behind is probably original to the railway. (P.J. Garland/Roger Carpenter)

Looking west in 1959 with more probably original stonework in evidence. (R.K. Blencowe)

The station seen from track level on 20 July 1963. The platform support stonework may again be original. (W.G. Sumner)

Looking east from the east end of the platform, showing the yard sidings and signal box in the centre on 21 May 1963. (P.J. Garland/ Roger Carpenter)

Whitland's No. 4132 running into Pembroke with the Pembroke Dock portion of the 11.55am from Paddington on 20 July 1963. Due at 7.8pm, this was a journey time of 7hrs. 13mins. from London. (W.G. Sumner)

2251 Class 0-6-0 No. 2287, transferred to Whitland after many years at Ebbw Jn., returns light from Pembroke Dock to Whitland after working the 11.55am Shrewsbury to Pembroke Dock. This was after a good day's work for an 0-6-0, starting by running from Whitland to Pembroke Dock, then working through to Llandeilo on the up Shrewsbury service, then back through to Pembroke Dock on the return Shrewsbury, and LE home. (W.G. Sumner)

A local train from Whitland calls at Pembroke on 1 June 1961 but there is little evidence of much business other than to unload empty milk churns. (L.R. Freeman/Transport Treasury)

56XXs had a long history in small numbers on the line. With a tractive effort of 25,800lbs, they were more powerful even than the 5101 Class, but were not good engines on passenger work if passenger comfort was concerned due to the pronounced fore and aft motion when steam was cut off. Here No. 6680 has arrived at Pembroke with the 10.45am from Whitland on 1 June 1961. (L.R. Freeman/Transport Treasury)

Another 56XX working on the line was No. 6623 seen here marshalling a goods train in Pembroke Yard on 1 June 1961.
(L.R. Freeman/ Transport Treasury)

The 460 yard long Golden Hill (or Pembroke) Tunnel between Pembroke and Pembroke Dock as on 21 May 1963.
(P.J. Garland/Roger Carpenter)

43xx No. 7332 on the three coach Pembroke Dock portion of the 8.55am from Paddington between Pembroke and Pembroke Dock on 9 August 1963.
(Gerald T. Robinson)

Between Pembroke Dock and Pembroke, Whitland's No. 5545 heads the 3.50pm from Pembroke Dock to Whitland on 9 August 1963, a 3 coach formation with parcels vans at both ends. (Gerald T. Robinson)

Not the wanted welcome to Wales as the 08.45 SO Paddington to Pembroke Dock runs into a storm as it passes through Pembroke station on 8 September 2018 with PC 43158 leading and 43122 trailing. The nature of West Wales weather is that by the time the train arrived at Pembroke Dock, the sun could be shining. (Stephen Miles)

PEMBROKE DOCK

The earliest plan of Pembroke Dock is for 1899, by when the layout was much the same as existed afterwards. Though Pembroke Dock was the end of the line for passenger trains, the line continued west into the docks and there was originally a Dockyard Extension Railway which was taken over by the Admiralty on 1 January 1892. This ran from the crossover at the end of the passenger station down to the dockyard, passing over several level crossings, some being Water Street, King Street, Gravel Lane and Commercial Row near which was a goods shed.

A third of a mile east of Pembroke Dock station, Llanion Halt had existed between 1 May 1905 and 1 October 1908. Just west of this halt was a line running north-west to Hobbs Point, located at West Lanion Pill, used as an Army Ordnance Siding and brought into use as such about 1911, with a PSA dated 19 October 1910 in the name of the Secretary of State for War. Near the junction for Hobbs Point, on the south side of the line, was an engine shed and turntable, and beyond the junction on the north side of the line was a goods yard with a goods shed.

Pembroke Dock station had two platforms, the main platform originally being longer than the other. A signal box was located at the east end of the main platform. In 1902, large scale alterations were made to the facilities available at the east end of the complex. The signal box was renewed, carriage sidings were provided alongside the line to Hobbs Point, coaling facilities for engines were improved, the turntable moved to the other side of the line, and the No.2 platform extended to be of equal length with No.1.

A down siding had been added east of the engine shed in 1915. In 1921 one of the sidings at Hobbs Point was leased to Amethyst Syndicate Ltd. and the Wales Gas Board had a PS off the goods yard which ceased in 1963 and was removed.

In 1942 additional siding accommodation was provided on the up side east of the engine shed.

The engine shed was closed in September 1963 when DMUs took over the operation of the line. The carriage sidings and engine facilities alongside the Hobbs Point line were also taken out of use at this time. The line to Hobbs Point was taken out of use on 4 January 1969 and the line beyond the station to the dockyard on 5 September 1971. The signal box had been reduced to a ground frame on 24 August 1966 and by the early 1970s little existed other than tracks into the platform.

With the service worked by DMUs which did not require turning or servicing, other than cleaning, fuelling being carried out elsewhere, and the withdrawal from the wagonload business in 1976, the infrastructure was drastically reduced, leaving only the two platform lines and a run-round facility if needed. In the course of time, the service has required only one platform and this is all that remains at Pembroke Dock in the present day. The station area has deteriorated, the redundant track site becoming overgrown and the station presents an unattractive, sad scene to the traveller.

Though the development of the Station Inn facility is to be much welcomed, money needs to be spent on the presentation of the working element of the station, which, other than Tenby, is the principal station on the line. Let us hope that the years that come hold a better future for this service which has been allowed to deteriorate in many respects. A minimum service of one train an hour is needed to maintain public interest in branch line services such as this, if they are to succeed into the future. With low operating costs in the use of modern two car DMUs, let us hope that the planners can provide an attractive service for modern times.

Approaching Golden Hill Tunnel, Bulldog 3729 (later 3439) with an up express. (P.Q. Treloar Collection)

The terminus station of Pembroke Dock with its two platforms. A 4575 Class 2-6-2T is starting a return train to Whitland from the main platform on 23 May 1958. (N.C. Simmons/ Hugh Davies)

A view along the main platform to the end of the line, with a starting service standing in Platform 2 on 21 May 1963. (P.J. Garland/Roger Carpenter)

Above left: The end of the journey for the Pembroke Dock portion of the 8.55am from Paddington, arriving at Pembroke Dock behind 61XX No. 6118 after a journey of 7hrs. 22mins. on 21 May 1963. (P.J. Garland/Roger Carpenter)

Above right: Double heading was quite common on the line either to return unbalanced engines to Whitland or for load. Here No. 4169 is coupled chimney to chimney with a fellow 41XX to return home on 14 September 1957. (F.K. Davies)

The only Class 1 service on the branch was the Pembroke Coast Express which called at all stations and took 1hr. 20mins. to reach Whitland, some of the Class 2 services being faster! Here two views of Neyland's No. 5357, working from Whitland, in charge in 1957.
(D.K. Jones Collection)

Manors became a mainstay of the line with the 41XX and 45XX 2-6-2Ts in the 1960s and here No. 7825 *Lechlade Manor* stands at the arrival platform, ready to reverse out on 15 November 1961. (D.K. Jones Collection)

A 4575 Class, 5520, paired with a 2251 Class, has just arrived at Pembroke Dock in June 1959, having worked together throughout from Whitland due to the load being too great for the 0-6-0 alone. (D.K. Jones Collection)

The stonework building at the end of the arrival platform is well shown in this shot of Carmarthen Manor No. 7826 *Longworth Manor* ready to reverse out of the departure platform with its train, while a departing train stands at the arrival platform on 26 June 1963. (C.M. & J.M. Bentley)

The crossover and shunt spur just beyond the platforms, leading into the single line to the Dockyard on 21 May 1963. This area was operated by the West Ground Frame. (P.J. Garland/Roger Carpenter)

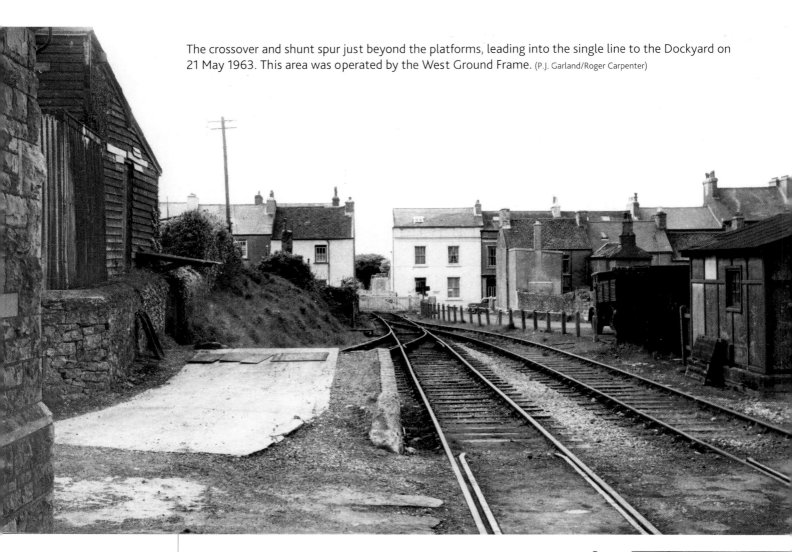

Beyond the platforms on the line to the Dockyard, there were two LCs. Here is the first one on 2 September 1959 with a road leading to the west end of the Goods yard. (R.K. Blencowe)

Three views of Pembroke Dock engine shed, a 2-track building extended in 1932 and closed in September 1963. The shed was equipped with a turntable capable of turning a 4-6-0. (P.J. Garland/Roger Carpenter)

Four views in the yard, the first showing former Birkenhead 2-6-2T No. 4122, the second No. 5571 shunting stock, both on 9 June 1962, the third 5180 in the shed yard and the fourth a view of running lines and siding with No. 4699 near the signal box and a 56XX (top right) shunting the train on the siding on 1 June 1961. (R.K. Blencowe x 2, C.M.& J.M. Bentley, L.R. Freeman/ Transport Treasury)

4132 with the 11.25am to Paddington at Platform 2 on 20 July 1963, with local stock on the front to be detached at Whitland. (W.G. Sumner)

5545 shunts parcels vans in the sidings on 20 July 1963. (W.G. Sumner)

4132 propels ECS off the 11.55am from Paddington into the sidings for cleaning and C&W attention before their return journey on 20 July 1963. (W.G. Sumner)

4132 had arrived at the down platform on the 11.55am ex-Paddington on 20 July 1963 and had been shunted to the departure platform en route to the sidings. (W.G. Sumner)

Two views of the exterior of Pembroke Dock station, the first on 1 June 1961. (L.R. Freeman/Transport Treasury. Great Western Trust)

The Pembroke Coast Express at the start of its journey to Paddington with Carmarthen Manor No. 7804 *Baydon Manor* at the head. This was the only Class 1 service on the line, though the timing to Whitland was slower than some Class 2s. The four coach train would attach the dining four car portion at Swansea, dep. 3.45pm, Cardiff 5pm and run non-stop from Newport arriving Paddington at 7.45pm, the fastest train of the day beyond Swansea. (L.R. Freeman/Transport Treasury)

6680 has arrived at Pembroke Dock with the 10.45am from Whitland on 1 June 1961. (L.R. Freeman/ Transport Treasury)

Before Manors took over the working of the Pembroke Coast Express in both directions between Carmarthen and Pembroke Dock, we see No. 5180 ready to depart with the train from the main platform at Pembroke Dock on 12 September 1959. (F.K. Davies)

4107 shunting empty main line stock for the 11.55am to Whitland on 28 May 1961. (Alan Wild)

Two long distance trains await departure from Pembroke Dock with No. 3214 on the 9.30am to Shrewsbury which it will work through to Llandeilo and No. 4132 on the 10.20am to Paddington on 7 July 1962. (Alan Wild)

No. 4122 with the 11.55am to Paddington on 27 May 1962 at Platform 2. (Alan Wild)

4107 with the three coach portion of the 11.55am from Paddington at the main platform on 7 July 1962. (Alan Wild)

Looking west along the stonework buildings on the arrival platform on 28 May 1961. (Alan Wild)

Summer Saturdays brought HSTs to the line for through working to and from Paddington as here on 2 June 1990. (Stuart Warr)

The Class 120 DMUs were the normal motive power for the Pembroke Dock services until the mid-1980s. Here are two shots of unit C504 (the C denoting a Cardiff Canton set) seen from both ends of Pembroke Dock platform. (Stuart Warr)

Top: Steam or diesel specials sometimes ran over the Pembroke Dock branch as part of Sunday West Wales tours. Here Pathfinder Tours' Pembrokeshire Pageant special from Coventry to Pembroke Dock and Fishguard, returning to Bristol 1Z33, runs into Pembroke Dock on 2 August 1997 behind two Class 37s, 37274 and 37686, the line now bordered by trees and other vegetation, showing up the difference between the railway in that area in the 1960s and the end of the century. (Stuart Warr)

Left: Following the introduction of new Class 150 and 153 DMUs, the 13.05 service to Swansea stands at Pembroke Dock worked by 153361 (leading) and 150253 on 1 September 2007. (Stuart Warr)

The 13.09 to Swansea stands at the platform on 18 March 2014. (Stuart Warr)

The exterior of Pembroke Dock station, part of which is now the Station Inn, on 18 March 2014. (Stuart Warr)

In the current livery, the 08.45 HST from Paddington stands at Pembroke Dock on 1 September 2018 with PC 43171 leading. Note the track is now lifted from the other platform line. (Stuart Warr)

A final view of the line's doyen service in the steam era, the name from which is still carried by steam and diesel specials to the line. Carmarthen's 7829 *Ramsbury Manor* waits to start the up Pembroke Coast Express from Pembroke Dock on 21 August 1962. (Colour Rail)

The 10.01 SO Summer Saturday Pembroke Dock to Paddington Pembroke Coast Express HST, with Power Car 43020 leading and 43053 on the rear, passes Llanion Crossing Pembroke Dock as it starts its journey to London on 8 September 2018. (Stephen Miles)

The current modern situation in summer as Power Car 80034 heads the GWR 08.45 from Paddington into Pembroke Dock 1B15 station at 14.08, hopefully setting a precedent for the future on 8 June 2019. (Stephen Miles)